PVA
glue

Scrap
Paper

cardboard
tubes and boxes

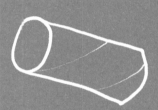

Notebook

(lots!)

Pencils
(stumpy ones are
useful
too)

Ruler

Big
Pens

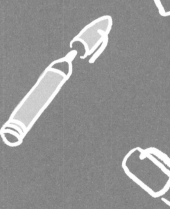

This is a first edition.
Welcome to your Awesome Robot is © 2013 Flying Eye Books.
All artwork and characters within are © Viviane Schwarz.

Published by Flying Eye Books, an imprint of Nobrow Ltd.
62 Great Eastern Street, London, EC2A 3QR.

Printed in the UK.
ISBN: 978-909263-00-0

Order from www.flyingeyebooks.com

The Base Unit

Your robot will arrive ready for upgrades.

 Keep away from fire.

Motion

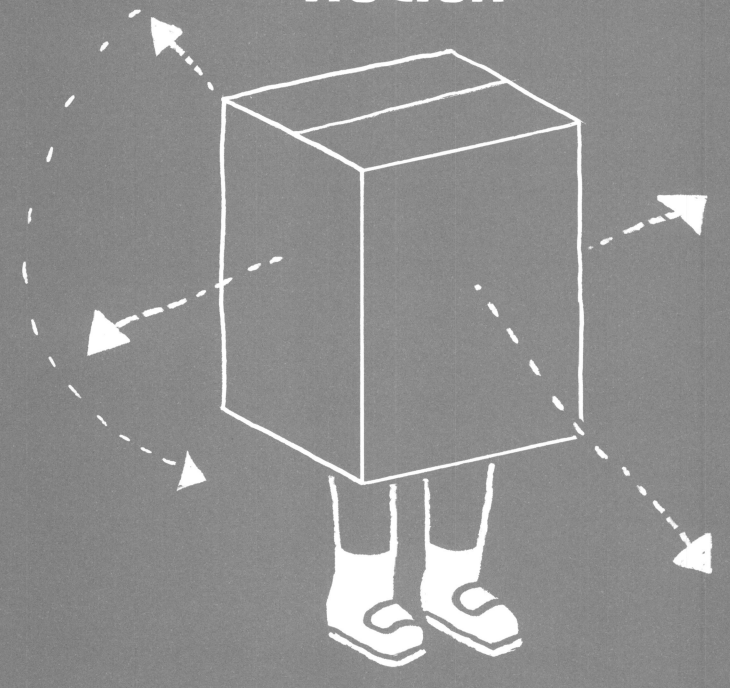

TO TEST MOTION:

Put your robot into operational position.

⚠ Do not test your robot near stairs or steep drops.
Stair climbing mode is NOT enabled on delivery.

⚠ Always test your robot in the presence of an assistant to prevent accidental damage.

GO!

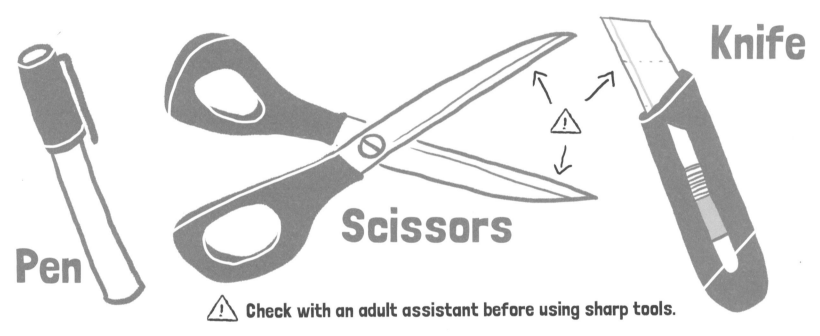

Pen

Scissors

Knife

⚠ Check with an adult assistant before using sharp tools.

Vision

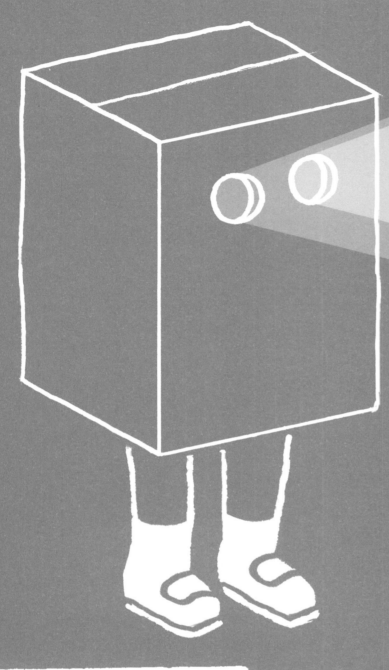

SOME STYLES:

 Stereoscopic

 Cyclops

 Panorama

 Full Interface

Locate suitable position for visor.

Cut visor hole(s).

Test visor.

If necessary, re-close and re-cut visor holes in different location.

⚠ Always empty your robot before cutting. **DO NOT CUT** while robot is operational.

⚠ Employ assistant for cutting.

Input/Output

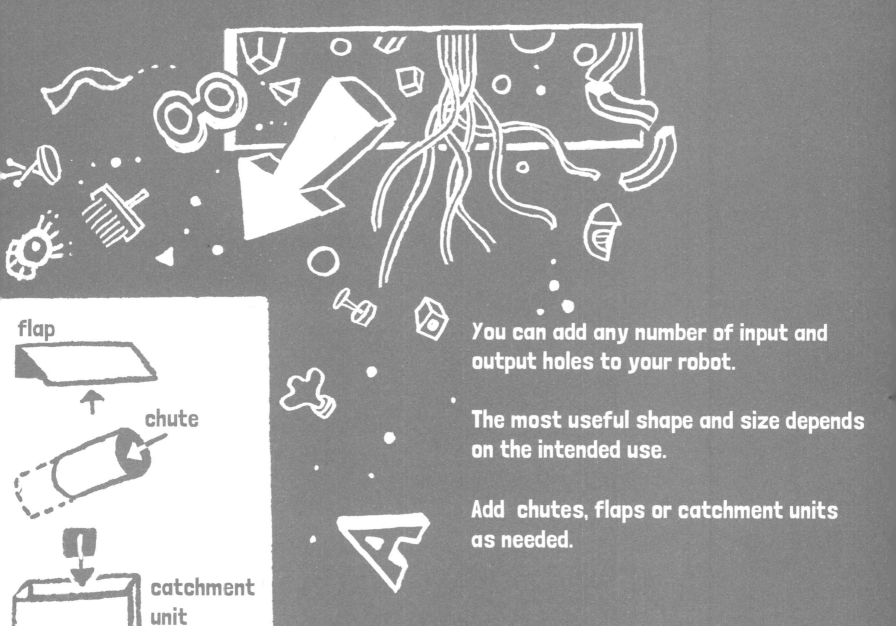

You can add any number of input and output holes to your robot.

The most useful shape and size depends on the intended use.

Add chutes, flaps or catchment units as needed.

flap

chute

catchment unit

Labels (Examples)

Insert
Fuel
Here

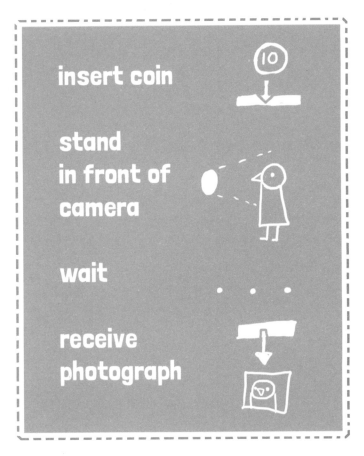

insert coin

stand
in front of
camera

wait

receive
photograph

DEATH RAY

Danger of Death

Confectionary
Quality
Control
Unit

OF COURSE!

MESSAGES

Scratching

Cargo Bucket
Handle with care

Serial Number

Name

Construction Date

Engineer

STAND BACK

This is a dancing robot

Intergalactic Exploration Vehicle

I'm not going to cut them from the book. My own are better... except maybe the Death Ray.

Snip Snip
Snip

Duct Tape...

... is the correct tool for the job.
Duct tape is very useful in engineering.
Always have plenty to hand.

Internal Storage

You may wish to install internal storage inside your robot.

⚠ Do not store sharp or otherwise dangerous materials.

 Note: Do not store animals, especially not <u>cats</u>.

HOW TO MAKE A DISPLAY DIAL

OUTSIDE   **INSIDE**

Use a strong piece of string.
Thread everything up in this order, then tighten the string, tie a knot and fix with tape.

Stumpy pencil (or similar)

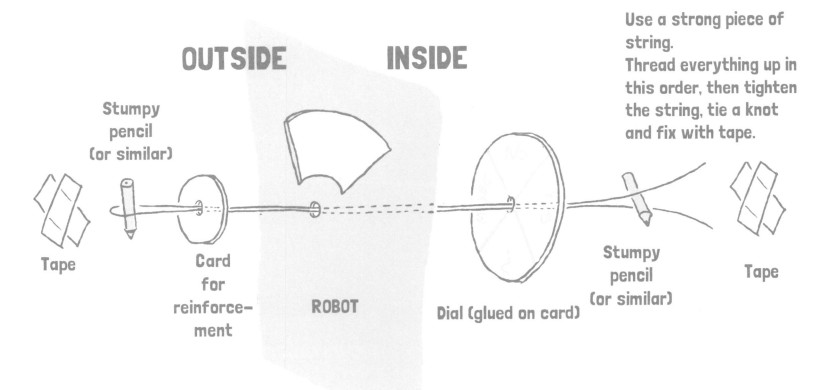

Tape

Card for reinforcement

ROBOT

Dial (glued on card)

Stumpy pencil (or similar)

Tape

The finished dial:

From inside your robot, it looks like this:

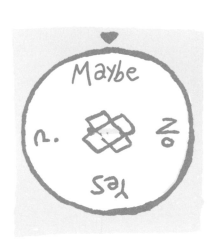

Displays

ACTIVATED

DIFFERENT DESIGNS

A simple binary display with moving arrow

A display can show important information about your robot's status.

Think about what your robot needs to communicate to the world.

If you make a display that can be changed from the OUTSIDE, it can be used to give commands to your robot.

0   LOW   MELT DOWN
                    DANGER

A sliding meter

← how is this one supposed to work??

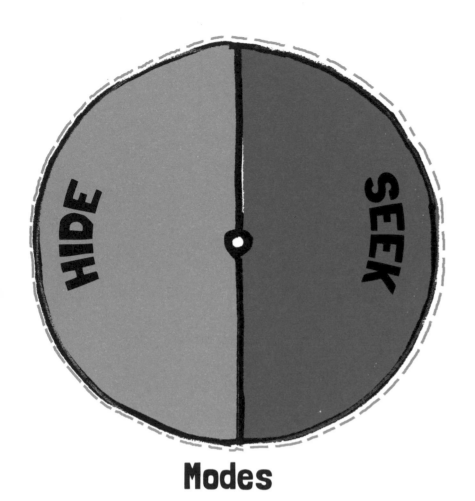

Modes

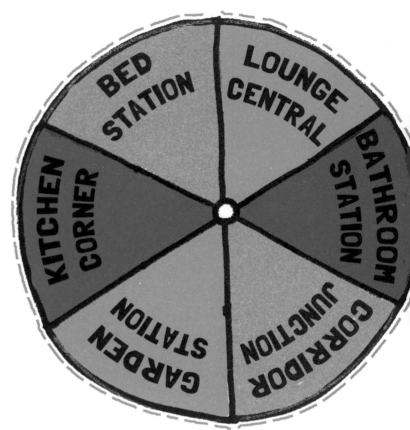

Regular Route Announcements

Output Select

Scanner

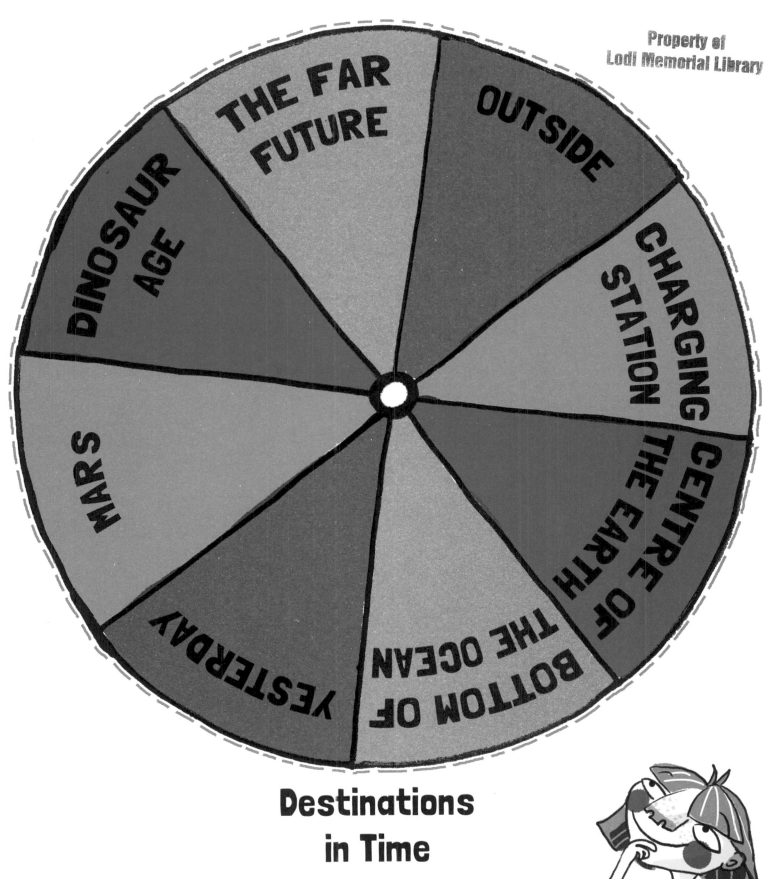

THE FAR FUTURE

OUTSIDE

DINOSAUR AGE

CHARGING STATION

MARS

CENTRE OF THE EARTH

YESTERDAY

BOTTOM OF THE OCEAN

**Destinations
in Time
and Space**

Attachments

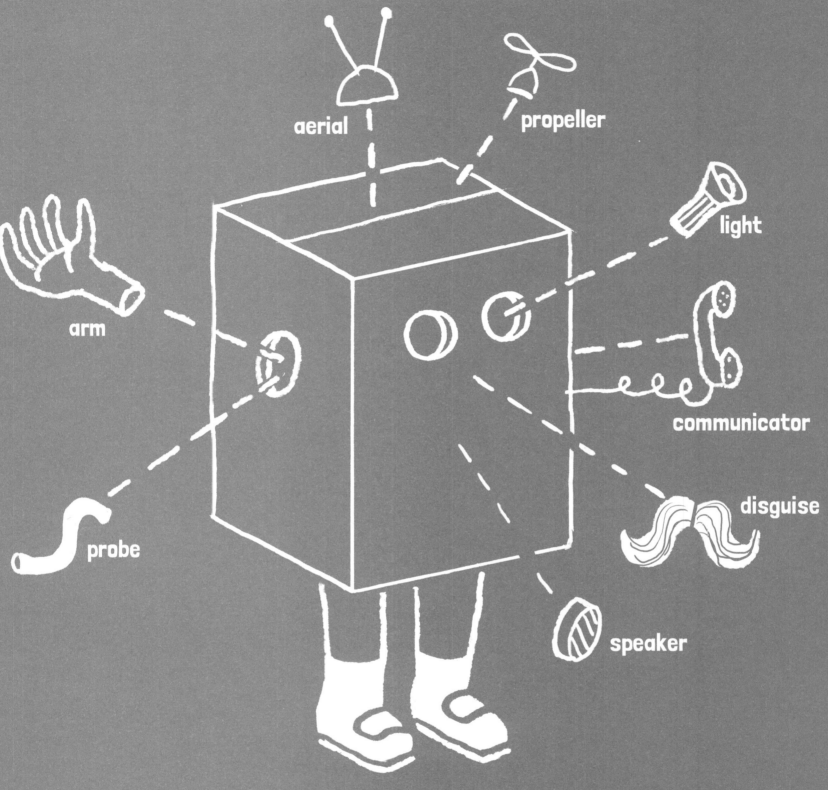

There are many additional parts available for your robot.

Look around your home. Go on missions to find new robot parts.

Experiment. Change them around. You can have new attachments for every situation!

⚠ NEVER attach dangerous parts, or use parts that belong to other people without their permission.

The Brain

The brain is the central component of your robot.

Use it to design any further upgrades you desire.

WORKSHOP RULES

for Engineers, Assistants & those around them

BEFORE YOU BEGIN:

Make an agreement about how and when to use the workshop and STICK TO IT.

1. NEVER damage the workshop.

2. ALWAYS tidy up your own work.

3. DON'T tidy away other people's work (unless they left it after the agreed time).

4. BE CONSIDERATE - warn people about things that may bother them (bad smells, loud noises).

5. DON'T use other people's things (unless they give you permission).

6. If you are not COMPLETELY SURE that something is SAFE - ASK an adult.

7. If anything looks dangerous, STOP AND TELL AN ADULT AT ONCE.

AND REMEMBER:

IT IS EVERY ENGINEER'S RIGHT TO DO THINGS BADLY WHILE WORKING THEM OUT!

Offer help and advice, make sure all is safe, but respect the engineer and don't interfere with their work.

Remove this page from the manual.
On the other side is a poster for your workshop.

Responsible Assistant

This is to certify that

....

has been invaluable in helping to design, build and test an

AWESOME ROBOT

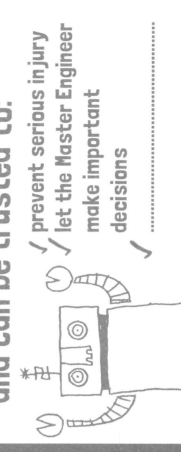

and can be trusted to:

- ✓ prevent serious injury
- ✓ let the Master Engineer make important decisions
- ✓ ....

Signed ....
(Master Robot Engineer)

Master Robot Engineer

This is to certify that

....

has successfully designed, built and tested an

AWESOME ROBOT

and can be trusted with the following:

- ✓ Scissors
- ✓ Duct Tape
- ✓ Robot
- ✓ ....
- ✓ ....
- ✓ ....

Signed ....
(Responsible Assistant)

Your robot is finished? Congratulations!
Remove these certificates from the manual.
Fill them in, have them signed and framed.

Notes

String (strong!)

Duct Tape

Scissors

Craft knife
(careful!)

Paint

Brushes